OFFICE SMARTS

252 Tips for Success in the Workplace

by
Roy J. Blitzer

The Globe Pequot Press

Old Saybrook, Connecticut

Text design by Saralyn D'Amato

Library of Congress Cataloging-in-Publication Data

Blitzer, Roy J.
    Office smarts : 252 tips for success in the workplace / by Roy J. Blitzer. — 1st ed.
        p. cm.
    ISBN 1-56440-386-6
    1. Vocational guidance. 2.Vocational guidance—Quotations, maxims, etc. 3. Office politics—Quotations, maxims, etc. 4. Interpersonal relations—Quotations, maxims, etc. I. Title.
    HF5381 . B464 1994
    650. 1—dc20   94-15873
                                                                      CIP

Manufactured in the United States of America
First Edition/Second Printing

Dedication

For my wife, Carol, and my daughters,
Mara and Hannah,
whose advice and love help me every day,
whether I go to work or not

Don't take yourself or the tips that follow too seriously—you'll lose your edge.

READ ON.

Don't stress out about **1**
things you can't control.

Return all phone calls. **2**

Use your energy and **3**
intelligence as if all
results depended on
you.

4 Give recognition and credit as if results depended only on others.

5 Support and make your boss look good in public. Provide needed feedback in private.

Choose a profession **6**
you love. Don't be
afraid to express your
passion.

Be visible by overwork- **7**
ing the first few months
at a new job. You'll
be perceived as a hard
worker much longer
than that.

8 If you don't know the answer, know where to find it. Have access to a company directory at all times.

9 Keep a simple "mindless" project available for phone holds and airport down times.

Remember to say **10**
please and thank you.

Do some copying, **11**
answering phones, and
making coffee. It makes
you appreciate those
who do it on a regular
basis, and it makes
them appreciate you.

12 Volunteer for nonprofits or community service and share your expertise. Both you and the company will look and feel better.

13 Buy at least one expensive suit. Vary your look with many different blouses or shirts and ties.

When you plan to be out **14**
of the office, tell your
assistant or co-worker
where you will be and
when you expect to
return.

Ask why you didn't get **15**
what you wanted
—graciously.

16 Carry your business card everywhere. Never be bashful about distributing it.

17 If you have committed to a follow-up meeting, hold to it. Cancellations signal a lack of interest and can erode trust.

18

Keep your shoes shined and your nails clean.

19

Spend the company's money as if it were your own. Err on the side of living carefully, but do not be foolishly tight-fisted.

20 At a business meal, be sensitive to who's paying. Don't order a more expensive item than your host.

21 Try to understand what's motivating the person giving you a tough time.

For every complaint you **22** make, have a possible solution or recommendation.

Think twice before **23** ordering alcohol at lunch. Take your drink signals from the senior person with you.

24 Be aware of corporate politics but don't participate.

25 Keep confidences but remember that not everyone does.

26 Avoid wearing too much perfume or cologne.

Be on time—maybe a **27**
few minutes early—
for all business
engagements. Arrive at
parties fashionably late.

Never miss a deadline. **28**
If it looks like you're
going to be late, negoti-
ate and change it. If you
can't change it, get help.

29 Take a few risks. It's better to be shot out of the water occasionally than to rot at the dock.

30 Seek out and pursue opportunities to write and publish in your area of expertise.

31

Keep your resume current, no longer than one page, and always have it available.

32

Don't give complicated directions by phone. Create a simple map showing how to get to your office and fax or mail it.

33 Try to do at least one thing you like each day.

34 Join and actively participate in trade organizations, councils, or professional associations. Volunteer for one key assignment.

Anticipate voice mail **35** when initiating business calls and prepare to deliver a clear, succinct message that includes your name, return phone number, and the time and date of your message.

36 When giving your name and phone number, speak slowly and distinctly. Spell your name, too, even if it's Smyth.

37 Seek and gain permission prior to using someone as a professional or personal reference.

Find out whether your **38** telephone call is welcome or intrusive. Ask if it's a good time to talk.

Be objective, clear, and **39** honest when recommending an individual or firm—your credibility is at stake.

40 Avoid discomfort and conflict by not discussing politics, religion, or salary.

41 Let your references know when you've applied for a new position and who might be contacting them for that reference.

Get exercise wherever **42** you are: Walk on the escalator or moving sidewalks, take the stairs rather than the elevator, walk to lunch, etc.

Eat lightly on airplanes **43** (you can order "special" meals) and avoid alcohol when in the air.

44 Allow time for someone to consider a problem. Don't insist on immediate solutions.

45 Don't keep visitors with appointments waiting when they come to call (five minutes at most).

Keep a toothbrush and **46**
toothpaste in your desk
and use them. (Floss, as
well.)

Reach an understanding **47**
with your boss about
how much time a
project should require
before undertaking it.

48 Buy one tux or one elegant evening dress.

49 At business meals, order foods that are easy to eat and that do not impede conversation. Avoid finger foods, pizza, and spaghetti.

Build in some stress- **50**
relieving fun on business
trips—a museum, movie,
show, etc.

Know how to operate all **51**
the office equipment you
use. If you use machines
only occasionally and
tend to forget, make crib
sheets.

52 Know how to maintain key office equipment—how to add toner to the copy machine, how to replace paper in the printer, etc.

53 Carry your jewelry, or anything important to you, on your person, never in your luggage.

Communicate with eye **54** contact. Always look the person in the eye, whether you're involved in a heavy negotiation or handing off an assignment to a staff member.

55 If possible, carry on all luggage, including briefcase, laptop, and hanging clothes.

56 Don't play phone tag or phone games. Let people know when you're available.

Buy rack suits and **57** have them tailored professionally.

Solicit criticism and **58** accept it without being defensive.

Never be afraid to **59** say "I'm sorry" or "I apologize."

60 Summarize what really went on in meetings for those not present (shifts in priorities, your interpretation of interpersonal dynamics, etc.).

61 Have enough cash on hand for a fine meal for two.

With new assignments, **62**
check back periodically
to see if you're on the
right track.

Don't be afraid to pick **63**
up a tab or ask, "How
do you want to handle
this bill?"

64 Before beginning any key discussion, clearly state the purpose, desired outcome, and key objective.

65 Keep up to date on the latest technologies. Learn as much as you can about new developments.

At the beginning of **66** each meeting, set an agenda, indicating approximate time to be spent on each item, and adhere to it.

Praise the team. Share **67** responsibility for both wins and losses.

68 Don't buy auto insurance when you rent a car if you are already covered. (Most companies have insurance for—or self insure—employees on company business.)

69 Don't guess or assume if you don't know.

The medium is the mes- **70**
sage. Pick a car that
makes a statement about
you (for example,
reliability).

Offer to bring a beverage **71**
to your co-worker when
getting one for yourself.

72 Find a laundry service that will deliver your blouses and shirts on hangers. (Boxed shirts often show creases.)

73 Know at least two good wines. Generally, the middle-priced ones on a restaurant wine list are the best value.

Keep the inside and outside of your car clean. (Dark colors show more dust in California, light colors in Pittsburgh.) **74**

Know how many pages you can fax before it becomes more economical to use an overnight courier service. **75**

76 Never sleep with a client or co-worker (no sex whatsoever).

77 Don't be afraid to "blow your own horn" (occasionally and gently) within the company, but be prepared to back it up.

Raise everyone's educational and interest level by distributing that timely article, clever quotation, etc. **78**

Don't promise performance unless you can deliver. **79**

80 Don't feel indebted to your employer. Your paycheck should reflect your contribution.

81 Take some office work home with you. You never know when there'll be an emergency.

Avoid giving personal **82**
financial counsel to
work associates.

Be sure your briefcase **83**
contains address labels,
stamps, stationery, and
overnight express
envelopes.

84 Practice tough inter-personal discussions in advance; it helps the real interaction go smoother. Anticipate variations.

85 Admit your error immediately. Report it to the person who can solve or repair it the fastest.

Visualize your success. **86**

87
Deal with the press
honestly and promptly
(same day). If required,
check with internal
authorities before
responding. Try to have
a statement prepared.

88 Keep a pad and pencil at your bedstand for capturing clever ideas and insights.

89 There is an exception to every rule. Push the limit when it's really important to you.

Keep a neat office and **90**
a tidy desk. A messy
environment could
influence people's
perceptions of you.

Learn how to use a **91**
Dictaphone and speak
in full sentences.

92 Don't be afraid to ask questions.

93 Listen carefully at meetings and contribute meaningfully when you speak.

94 Never fudge an expense report.

Be careful about **95**
socializing too much
with employees who
report directly to you.
Friendship problems
could interfere with the
professional business
relationship.

96 Never tear or mutilate papers you are throwing away. Toss them whole into the waste basket just in case you need to retrieve them later on in the day. Better yet, keep them in the recycle bin.

Remember birthdays of **97**
your co-workers and try
to know at least one
other piece of personal
data about each of them.

Always write a personal **98**
thank-you note for
special favors within
two days.

99 Keep records easily accessible. Err on the side of saving too much.

100 Don't say a co-worker has a bad "attitude." Describe the specific behavioral detail that annoys you.

Create as many strands **101**
to your life as you can.
Get active in group-
oriented activities; for
example, coach or play
on a team, participate
in a musical group,
or become a scout
leader.

102 Answer the phone within three rings.

103 Don't interrupt your answering machine. Listen to the entire message before returning the call.

104 Back up computer data often.

Never make a business **105**
call during the dinner
hour; leave that to the
solicitors.

Set realistic goals and **106**
have high expectations
for accomplishing
them.

107 Remember, everyone has a bad day now and then. Be tolerant.

108 Write up meeting notes and key discussion agreements as soon as possible, while details are still fresh in your mind.

Use gridded flip-chart **109**
paper for stand-up pre-
sentations. Your charts
will be easier to create
and read.

When praising an **110**
employee in writing,
send a copy to the
individual's boss.

111 Double check all hotel wake-up call requests.

112 Sign up for at least one professional develop-ment experience per year. Pay for it yourself if necessary.

Use a pay phone at the **113**
airport to deal with can-
cellations or problems
with connecting flights.
It's often faster than
waiting in line with the
other disappointed
passengers.

114 Never use a company fax machine for anything that's private or confidential.

115 Have a cute noncontroversial joke ready to break the ice.

If you travel frequently, **116**
carry an up-to-date
pocket airline guide for
last-minute changes.

Carry a portable **117**
steamer or iron to
eliminate wrinkles
before key out-of-town
appointments.

118 Date every document you receive and send.

119 Never call anyone collect. It makes you look cheap!

120 Never trust your memory when setting up appointments. Always write them down.

A reference is a **121** knowledgeable recommendation for someone whose abilities you know well. A referral is a courtesy nod for an acquaintance who may want to use your name. Know the difference.

122 Never use business phones for long-distance personal calls or 900 inquiries.

123 If ever in doubt about an action, apply the television test: Would you be comfortable if this were broadcast on the six o'clock news?

Close every meeting **124**
with a summary of who
will do what by which
date.

Make certain you under- **125**
stand your assistant's or
co-worker's filing system
so you can find some-
thing in an emergency.

126 Carefully proofread everything that goes out with your signature on it.

127 Be cautious about what you say and how loudly you say it in a restaurant or hotel room. You never know who's nearby.

Keep your hands out of **128**
your pockets during
formal presentations or
speeches. Don't fiddle
with your pen either.

Pencils, pads, pens, etc. **129**
belong to the company.
Don't contribute to
white-collar crime.

130 Sustain your focus on what matters most. Try not to worry about unimportant tasks.

131 When you're negotiating a deal, "no" isn't "no" until it's been qualified four times.

Introduce yourself to **132**
your airplane seatmate
before starting your
work. She or he could
be a competitor—or an
interesting and useful
contact.

Being right and being **133**
effective are not always
the same.

134 In a sales setting, once you've asked for the order, be silent. Whoever speaks first loses.

135 Make sure more than one person knows where the fuse box is.

Use some kind of "time **136** manager" or daily planner to coordinate your priorities. Keep it visible.

Follow up all express- **137** mail or fax correspon- dence with a phone call to verify arrival.

138 Avoid prejudging future colleagues. You may find a so-called ogre delightful to work with if you approach the situation with your own fresh objectivity.

139 Tell the front desk when you have guests coming to visit.

Before asking for a salary **140** raise, make sure you document your case.

When flying from foggy **141** and snowy destinations in the winter, leave plenty of time for making contingency plans and connecting arrangements at the airport.

142 If you can, use professionally created overhead transparencies (with bold lettering and lots of white space) and laser-printed handouts. They can greatly enhance your presentation.

If your personal sched- **143**
ule permits, make your-
self popular by taking
your vacation when no
one else wants to.

Before a job interview **144**
begins, research the
company and learn
something about the
interviewer.

145 Exchange home phone numbers with your breakfast-meeting colleague in case there's a last-minute cancellation or unforeseen emergency.

146 Define the problem carefully before launching into solutions.

In your hotel room, **147**
check the T.V. and clock
radio alarms to avoid
unwanted disturbances
from previous guests'
settings.

When returning from **148**
trips, bring back a small
treat (candy, etc.) for the
staff left behind.

149 Find out the salary range of the position you're interested in before beginning the job-search process.

150 End each employee discussion on a positive note and, if necessary, with a specific time and follow-up date.

Conflict can bring posi- **151**
tive results. It's okay to
disagree constructively.

Postpone discussions **152**
when you are angry or
especially upset.
Emotional outbursts are
hard to repair, and it's
easier to be objective after
some time has elapsed.

153 Involve the employee in solving his or her own problem. Ask, "What do *you* think will help?"

154 Master the art of handling resistance by enrolling in a selling-skills seminar.

Never hire anyone at a **155** drastic salary reduction. Despite his or her protestations that "it doesn't matter," it will.

Set goals each year that **156** are measurable and time-based. Stretch yourself a bit, too.

157 Capture your speech or presentation audience by using a clever, inoffensive, noncontroversial quotation, story, or joke.

158 Distribute kitchen clean-up duties to *all* office personnel.

Use a to-do list every **159** day. Tackle the top priority—even if it's not the easiest—first.

Have a recent set of ref- **160** erence books available at all times (dictionary, thesaurus, style manual, etc.).

161 Make time to listen. For any discussion, hold calls and avoid interruptions that convey disinterest.

162 Assign projects to those who are interested in them and skilled to do them. Don't dump your garbage on the eager.

Be clear about your **163**
personal managerial
expectations. Define
what success looks like
to you and tell your
employees.

Before entering a seri- **164**
ous negotiation, decide
what you're willing to
give up.

165 Save a file of your recognition letters, special awards, and so on. Read the contents when you've had a bad day or need a lift.

166 Back up verbal complaints in writing if they concern issues particularly important to you.

In an employment **167** interview, come prepared with questions on budgets, long-term growth potential, perceptions of the department, etc. Good questions tell an effective interviewer just as much as good answers.

168 Keep local phone books, a zip-code directory, and a telephone area code listing easily accessible.

169 Refrain from giving personal advice to employees about home issues. Just listen and sympathize.

When offering feed- **170**
back, give concrete
specifics; for example,
"You fiddled with your
pen" instead of "You
seemed very nervous."
Keep it within the
control of the receiver.

Wear comfortable clothes. **171**

172 When listening to complaints, acknowledge the concerns. Most of us want to be heard as much as we want our complaint resolved.

173 Never sign a document on anyone's behalf without prior agreement.

Avoid making social **174** comparisons between employees who report to you. Evaluate against standards of conduct and performance.

Walk around your rental **175** car and look for dings before leaving the parking lot.

176 Document your employees' successes and note all key conversations and actions. They will come in handy when preparing for your performance discussion.

177 Write your name on whatever's yours in the office refrigerator.

Break your routine. **178**
Take a different route to
work or experiment
with new places for
lunch. Change in little
ways so the major ones
won't come as such a
shock.

179 Get receipts for all business expenses.

180 "Do you," "Can you," and "Are you able to" are closed questions and solicit a yes or no answer. Use them to close down a discussion or to move on.

What, Where, When, **181**
and *How* questions
open up the floodgates
for data gathering. Use
them to elicit informa-
tion or involvement.

Don't be afraid to put the **182**
high bid on the table, but
be realistic and open to
compromise.

183 Use your errors and mistakes as opportunities to learn. Ask, "How would I do this differently next time?" or "What did I learn?"

184 Compute your expense report on the airplane home, when details are fresh in your mind.

Try stress-management **185** techniques; they often work. For example, enjoy relaxing music during a car commute or catch a quick cat nap at lunch time. (For more suggestions, buy a book on the subject.)

186 Let some situations rest. It's not always productive or positive to rehash or process over and over.

187 Make sure your rental car's wipers, heater, spare tire, defroster, and radio are in working order before you leave the parking lot.

Negotiate the perks of **188** the position you're interviewing for— private office, special bonuses, salary increases, etc.—before the formal job offer is made. Get them in writing, if possible. They are harder to obtain later on.

189 When arranging a special business function, take the name of the restaurant employee handling the reservation. It indicates to the restaurant that your engagement is important.

Use round tables for all **190**
office meetings and
social functions, if
possible.

Beware of managers **191**
with open-door policies.
They often exhibit
closed minds.

192 Keep personal calls to an absolute minimum on company time/expense.

193 When traveling to a business meeting, never part with the clothes, toiletries, and accessories you need for your first appointment.

Before your trip, **194**
double-check all airline
tickets and hotel and car
reservations. Reconfirm
all return flights, and
save slips with confir-
mation numbers.

Check before forwarding **195**
someone else's voice-
mail message.

196 Understand the priorities of your job and never let the most important tasks slide.

197 Have drinks available to meet particular dietary or health restrictions of your guests (decaf coffee, herbal teas, juices, etc.).

Prepare for your **198**
holiday by leaving
detailed notes and
explanations. Use the
time away to relax
totally by not calling in
and worrying.

Know your employee **199**
benefits. Read all
literature thoroughly.

200 Think big picture and plan. There's truth to the expression, "Failing to plan is planning to fail."

201 Use a shredder for all confidential documents you wish no one to see. (And don't forget to take the data off your hard drive.)

202 Don't wait until the night before a project is due to learn a new software package. Try out the system with a simple, noncritical project first.

203 Don't abuse home telephone numbers. Try to conduct all your business at work.

204 To help with writer's block, try composing your document as if it were a letter to a favorite friend or relative.

205 Spend a few hours sorting the company mail one day, if possible. It tells you a lot about the organization.

Play to the "style" of your **206** key customers: Writers like memos; listeners like dialogues.

Send a postcard to the **207** person who is especially difficult to reach directly. Let him or her know you need to make contact and by what date.

208 Watch your language. Profanity may feel good to you at the moment, but to others it may signal limited vocabulary or lack of respect.

209 Know where the office supplies are kept or who has the keys to the supply cabinet.

Exit interviews are **210** important for you and for the organization. Retell only significant problems in a few key areas needing improvement—and don't burn any personal bridges.

211 Never assume your electronic voice-mail system matches that of the outside person you are calling. Each system is different, and a pound-key push can mean different things.

212 Save your favorite letters (even if you didn't write them). They can serve as models for future correspondence.

213 Standardize your key codes (bank ATM, computer call numbers, voice-mail password, etc.). This helps the memory a bit.

214 Avoid breaking your chain of thought when writing. If you are unsure of just the right word or of a spelling, put a big bold question mark in place of the word or phrase and get back to it later.

Take advantage of any **215**
available tax-deferred
savings plans. It benefits
you, and your employer
looks favorably on
participation.

Treat yourself to a **216**
massage.

217 Arrive early for a speech or presentation to check out the room setup and equipment (microphone, video, slide projector, overhead projector). Assume that what can go wrong, will.

218 If looking for group participation, ask a question and count to ten before moving on. The silence is worse for the group than it is for you.

219 When using someone else's office, be careful to return things to their original places.

220 Tape your name to your scissors, stapler, and other desk items. They are less likely to disappear that way.

221 Stretch at regular intervals throughout the day. It can ease tiredness and reduce tension.

Use water-based markers **222**
for charting. They don't
bleed through to the
next page.

Spend all of your **223**
budget before the end
of the year. If you have
carry-overs, you'll most
likely be cut the next year.

224 If possible, and practical, call home every night when you are away on business.

225 Cogitate for a day or so before taking action on major decisions. Time to digest or sleep on it is worth it in the long run.

Don't send a staff mem-**226**
ber on personal errands.
It can be demeaning.

Be aware of your **227**
colleagues' rules about
touching. When in
doubt, don't touch
anyone. Even a pat on
the shoulder can be
misinterpreted.

228 If you're bothering to take a phone message for a co-worker, make it accurate and complete.

229 Remember that Friday afternoon is the worst time to talk to anybody about anything important.

Listen to a book on **230** those long stretches of highway commuting.

Let your boss know if **231** you are talking to anyone above him or her. Procedural topics are okay. Policy issues are risky.

232 Never sit at the head of the table at a meeting. Position yourself within the group.

233 Be open and honest about what you think is your turf and its importance to you.

Use a task board with **234** magnets or Post-it notes to manage the flow of large projects.

Get a grip. Notice when **235** you're feeling tense or apprehensive and remind yourself of prior successes.

236 Take the time for group consensus ("buy-in") in decision making. The results are worth it.

237 Remember that the person shown favoritism will be the first one to foul up.

Change your voice-mail **238** message every day that you plan to be away from the office. People like to know your accessibility.

Never use put-down **239** humor to smooth over a conflict.

240 Be sensitive to labeling people, whether for race, religion, gender, or disability.

241 Make sure you understand your role in a project and how/where you fit into the plan. Be prepared to make changes.

To clarify a point, draw **242** a diagram or chart with labels. Clarity can quickly be brought to abstruse discussions by providing everyone with something to point to.

243 If you're not getting enough input or feedback, ask for it. For example, ask "How do you think that presentation went?"

244 When accepting advice or receiving feedback, consider the source.

One person should **245** never dictate group rewards. Brainstorm with the team to decide on appropriate ways to celebrate team milestones and mini successes.

246 Polish your listening skills. Show interest in what is being said to you. Ask questions to clarify confusion. Let the other person know you understand.

When interviewing poten- **247** tial employees, define the specific behaviors required and craft appropriate questions to match.

Your boss is your key **248** "customer." Discover early what objectives are most important and play to them.

249 Coordinate phone meetings carefully and be ready at the appointed time.

250 Keep deodorant, a toothbrush, and toothpaste in your briefcase (or easily accessible) to freshen up after long airplane flights.

Keep your boss in the **251**
loop and apply the "no
surprise" rule.

Admit your mistakes **252**
and forgive those of
others.

Acknowledgments

Thanks to many friends and family who were kind enough to read (test) my drafts and "trigger" improvements and additional suggestions. Their names appear below. Appreciation also to Laura Strom at Globe Pequot and Jeff Herman of the Jeff Herman Literary Agency for their support.

Andrew Cohen, Bob Leibenluft, Carl Davidson, Danice McGrew, David Gordon, Denise Leish, Earl Molander, Ellen Leibenluft, Hal Luft, Ian Tuller, J. J. Martin, Jack Goodkin, Jack Zenger, Jeannie Edwards, JoAnne Tybinka, Judy Walsh, Kathy Goodman, Lois Bernstein, Lori Luft, Marty Mazner, Nancy Alexander, Owen Griffiths, Paul Edwards, Peg Downey, Rene White, Richard Alexander, Ruth Mazner, Shira Luft, Steve Knight, Susie Richardson, Vicki Ryan

About the Author

Roy Blitzer is a corporate vice president and executive consultant of Zenger-Miller • Achieve, a management training and consulting organization in San Jose, California. He has previously held employee training and development positions with major corporations. In addition, he teaches classes in management and organizational behavior and writes articles on these subjects for professional magazines.

ORDER THIS BOOK
at a discount
for your friends, business associates, social group or club

For special discounts see your local bookseller,
or call toll-free 24 hours a day 1-800-243-0495 (in Connecticut,
call 1-800-962-0973) or write to

The Globe Pequot Press
P.O. Box 833
Old Saybrook
Connecticut, 06475-0833.

Also, for information on special discounts for corporate or other
large group sales, please contact John Chamberlain, Special Sales
Manager, The Globe Pequot Press.